The

4

Ingredients

Paleo

Cookbook

All The Recipes Have 4 Ingredients or Fewer!

Marjorie Kramer

Disclaimer

Books by Marjorie Kramer

1. The No-Cook, Skinny, Delicious, Nutritious Overnight Oats in a Jar Cookbook
2. The No-Cook, Skinny, Delicious, Nutritious, Oat Smoothies Cookbook
3. The 4 Ingredients Paleo Cookbook – All The Recipes Have 4 Ingredients or Fewer!
4. The 2 Ingredient Cookbook – All The Recipes Have Only 2 Ingredients!
5. The 2 Ingredient Dessert Cookbook – All the recipes have only 2 ingredients!
6. The 26 Worst Facebook Grammar Mistakes Ever & How to Avoid Them
7. Charting New Territory in ESL – What You Wish Your ESL Book Included

Introduction

I've been trying to pay more attention to what I eat, with an eye toward moving veerrryy sllooowwwllyy toward Paleo. One of my biggest problems is that I hate, no really, I hate to cook. Like I.hate.to.cook.

I went on a search to see what I could do about my problem, and voilà! Quick, easy, Paleo recipes with four ingredients or fewer! Fewer ingredients equals less time in the kitchen! How easy is that?

In here, you'll find something for everyone! There are recipes for breakfast, lunch, and dinner, delicious snacks, and some incredible recipes for desserts and sweets! Where do I sign up?!

Table of Contents

Banana Bacon Frittata

This delicious frittata has the smoky taste of bacon, and the sweetness of banana. Perfect!

Ingredients
  4 eggs
  1 ripe banana
  1 tbsp bacon fat
  Crumbled bacon to taste

Directions
  Over medium-high heat, melt the bacon fat in a medium pan.
  In your blender, mix together the eggs and banana until smooth.
  Pour the mixture into your pan.
  Crumble bacon bits on top.
  Cover the pan.
  Turn the heat to medium-low.
  Cook until the edges of the frittata begin to brown, and the egg is thoroughly cooked.

Fried Plantains

I first had fried plantains when I moved to Key West. They are unbelievably good! When you buy your plantains, remember that they need to be very black, no yellow left, when you cook them, so buy the ripest ones you can find.

Ingredients

2 very ripe, black, medium sweet plantains
butter, oil, or lard (!)

Directions

Peel the plantains, and cut them – either lengthwise or into 1-inch diagonal slices.
Put ¼" to ½" melted butter, oil, or lard in a pan over medium heat so that the oil is hot, but not burned.
Turn the heat to medium low, and put the plantains in. They should bubble nicely in the oil. Don't let them burn, or get too dark on the outside. The trick is to cook the inside without scorching the outside.
Cook about 10 – 15 minutes, turning once, or until golden brown.

Maple Soufflé

This is a perfect breakfast recipe for a weekend morning. Impress your significant other, or just pamper yourself with this yummy breakfast treat. Also a fantastic dessert!

Ingredients
> 2 eggs
> 1/3 cup maple syrup (Grade A Dark Amber is a good choice.)

Directions
> Preheat your oven to 400°F (204°C).
> Separate the eggs.
> In a small bowl, add the syrup to the egg yolks and whisk.
> In a stainless steel bowl, beat the egg whites until peaks form.
> Carefully fold the syrup and yolk mixture into the egg whites.
> Pour into four small bowls or ramekins, and place them on a baking sheet.
> Place the baking sheet in the 400°F (204°C) oven, and then immediately turn it down to 375°F (190°C). Bake until the soufflés are puffed, about 10 minutes.
> Enjoy!

Green Smoothie

You don't have to be afraid of this Green Smoothie! It tastes like a Piña Colada!

Ingredients

1 cup of frozen pineapple (You can buy a can of pineapple, transfer mostly the fruit with a little bit of juice to a cup, then put into a plastic container and freeze.)
¾ cup of coconut milk
1 cup of baby spinach

Directions

Put the coconut milk in your blender.
Add the baby spinach.
Purée until smooth.
Add your frozen pineapple.
Purée until smooth. Enjoy!

No-Flour Banana Pancakes

No flour! No Coconut flour, no almond flour, nothing!
Just two ingredients!

Ingredients
1 banana
2 eggs

Directions
Cut the peeled banana into several pieces.
Put the banana pieces and the two eggs into a
bowl.
Blend well.
Put a little coconut oil into a pan. Warm it over
medium-high heat.
Pour the mix in a spiral (this insures a thin
cake) into the pan, making whatever sized
pancakes you choose.
Let your pancakes cook on one side until you
see the bubbles and holes, about 10 minutes.
Flip carefully with a spatula. Without flour,
these pancakes are delicate. Cook another 10
minutes.
You can drizzle a little honey over these, but
really, they don't need a thing. They're very
sweet and delicious as is!

Possible additions/toppings
Almond Butter
Vanilla

Stevia
Cinnamon
Chocolate Chips
Cocoa Powder
Pumpkin
Berries

Baked Avocado and Egg

So easy, and so good! The basic recipe is 2 ingredients, avocado and eggs. Possible additions are at the bottom of this very simple recipe!

Ingredients
   1 ripe avocado
   2 small eggs

Directions
   Preheat your oven to 425°F (218°C).
   Slice the avocado in half, and remove the pit. If the resulting hole looks too small to contain an egg, take a bit out to enlarge the hole.
   Put each avocado half in a small baking dish or on a baking sheet. Make sure that the avocado is touching either one side of the dish, or the other avocado half. This keeps your breakfast steadier.
   Crack one egg into each avocado half. Try to get the yolk in first, so that if any egg spills out of the avocado, it will be the whites.
   Bake in your preheated oven about 15 – 20 minutes (depending on the size of the avocado and egg), or until the egg is cooked through.
   Remove, add any extras you want, and enjoy!

Possible additions
   crumbled cooked bacon
   sausage

grated cheese
tomato
salsa
cayenne pepper
chopped fresh chives or other fresh herbs
hot sauce

Egg Drop Soup

This is SO quick, and as tasty as you can get at a Chinese restaurant! Also way cheaper!

Ingredients
> 1 32-oz box or can of salted chicken stock
> 3 large eggs

Directions
> In a medium pot, bring the stock to a simmer.
> Crack the eggs into a bowl, and beat.
> Slowly dribble the eggs into the simmering stock, stirring constantly.
> After a couple seconds, it's done! Serve hot! Delicious!

French Fried Potatoes, Beets, Parsnips, or Carrots!

A great recipe for root veggies!

Ingredients

    root vegetables (potatoes, beets, parsnips, carrots)
    few tbsp Coconut Oil
    Sea salt

Directions

    Preheat your oven to 400°F (204°C)
    Cut your veggies up into thick "fries," about ½" thick.
    Put the veggie fries into a pan with the coconut oil and the sea salt for 5 minutes.
    Spread your veggies out in one layer on a parchment-lined cookie sheet.
    Bake for 25 minutes, take them out, turn them over, and bake for 20 more minutes.
    Enjoy!

Sweet Potato Chips

Not in the mood for fries? Try these chips!

Ingredients

    1 medium sweet potato, sliced into 1/8-inch thick slices
    1 tbsp cooking fat, melted
    ½ tsp sea salt

Directions

    Preheat your oven to 400°F (204°C).
    Slice the potato into very thin, 1/8" slices.
    Put the fat into a small bowl.
    Put each slice into the fat, then on a baking sheet. Don't overlap the slices.
    Bake for 11 minutes.
    Take out, and with a spatula, turn the chips over.
    Bake for another 11 or so minutes, until the edges are crisp.
    Take out and immediately sprinkle with sea salt.

Yummy!

Bacon- Wrapped Dates

Two of my favorite foods together!

Ingredients
    12 slices of bacon
    24 pitted Medjool dates

Directions
    Preheat your oven 350°F (176°C).
    Cut the bacon in half.
    Wrap half a piece of bacon around each date.
    Put each on a parchment paper-lined cookie
    sheet
    Bake for 20 minutes.
    Broil for 5 minutes.
    Cool for just a few minutes, stick a toothpick in
    each, and serve!

Optional
If you like, you can also slit the dates, and stuff
them with your favorite filling. Goat cheese or
mango chutney are a couple good ones.

Prosciutto-Wrapped Melon

Here's another recipe wrapping a fav fruit in a delicious meat!

Ingredients

¼ of a ripe cantaloupe

2 teaspoons white or gold balsamic vinegar (I know, I know. The purists say it's not Paleo, but some of the Paleo experts say it's OK in small amounts, as it is here.)

3-4 oz. thinly sliced prosciutto

Directions

Peel the melon, and remove the seeds.

Cut the melon into more slender segments, then cut those in half.

Put these into a bowl with the vinegar (Optional: add ½ tsp freshly ground black pepper and some very thinly-cut mint leaves.)

Cut or tear your sliced Prosciutto into strips, one to two inches wide.

Wrap each piece of cantaloupe with one or two strips of the Prosciutto.

Nothing to it, and mm-mm-mm!

Energy Bar

Delicious, and with only your pure ingredients!

Ingredients

 1 cup of your favorite roasted nuts
 1 cup of your favorite dried fruit
 a dozen or more whole, pitted dates

Directions

 Put the roasted nuts, dried fruit, and dates into your food processor.

 Pulse to break them up. If the dates clump together, separate them, and pulse some more.

 Press for 30 seconds, until everything is in crumbs.

 Press again for a minute or two, until the mixture becomes a ball.

 Put the mixture on a piece of plastic wrap, and work into a square about 8"x 8".

 Wrap, and chill for one hour to overnight.

 Unwrap the very chilled dough.

 On a cutting board, cut out bars to the size you want. Wrap each bar in plastic. They will keep in the fridge for weeks, or in the freezer for months.

 If you eat them cold, they will be chewy. As they warm, they will become softer.

Optional additions

chocolate chips
shredded coconut
cocoa powder
cinnamon
nutmeg
lemon or lime zest

Cranberry Sauce

One of the things I REALLY didn't want to give up when I started going Paleo was cranberry sauce. Love the stuff. With this recipe, I don't have to do without!

Ingredients

> 12 oz cranberries
> ¾ cup orange juice
> ½ cup honey

Directions

> Combine the ingredients in a pot.
> Simmer over medium heat.
> Berries will pop, and sauce will thicken in about 10 to 15 minutes.
> Cool completely off the burner.
> Refrigerate.

So easy for such a great side!

Coconut Butter-Stuffed Dates

Another date recipe!

Ingredients
      10 pitted dates
      1 cup coconut butter

Directions
      Soften the butter so that you can scoop it.
      Make a pocket in each date by slicing each slightly.
      Put a scoop of butter in each date

Serve and enjoy!

Caramels

What can you say but mmmmmmm…?

Ingredients
10 pitted, chopped Medjool Dates
1 tbsp ghee

Directions
Put the ghee in a pot on medium heat.
Add dates.
Sauté until the dates soak up almost all of the ghee, around five minutes.
Turn the mixture onto a sheet of parchment paper.
Put a second piece of paper on top.
Flatten the mixture with a plate or spatula.
Chill in the fridge for an hour.
Cut into squares.
Either chilled or at room temperature, it's fantastic!

Indian Crispy Chicken

Ingredients

5 chicken drumsticks
1 tbsp salt
1 - 2 tbsps garam masala
coconut oil for greasing baking dish

Instructions

Preheat your oven to 450F° (230°C).
Put the coconut oil in the baking dish.
In a bowl, combine the salt and the garam masala.
Rinse and lightly dry the drumsticks. If they're too wet, they won't get crispy.
One by one, put the drumsticks into the bowl and coat with the mixture.
Lay the drumsticks in the baking dish, not touching.
Bake for 40 minutes, or until crispy.

Fantastic!

Chicken Verde

Ingredients

1 lb boneless, skinless chicken thighs
8 ounces salsa verde

Directions

Add the chicken to your slow cooker.
Cover the chicken with salsa verde.
Cook on low for 5 hours.
If you like, you can open at 4 hours and pull the chicken apart with forks.
Put back in and finish cooking.

Optional
If you want to use the liquid in the slow cooker, you can thicken it before serving by reducing it in an uncovered pan, over medium-high heat.
If you like, you can brown the chicken either before or after cooking it in the slow cooker.

Buffalo Wings

Ingredients
chicken wings
1/3 cup Frank's Red Hot sauce (all natural)
2 tbsp butter
salt and pepper, paprika

Directions
Place the chicken wings on a cookie sheet
Sprinkle with the seasonings.
Bake at 400°F (204°C) for approximately 1 hour.
To make them crispy, drain the juices a couple of times while they're cooking.
In a pot on low heat, melt and whisk the butter and the hot sauce.
The wings should be crispy but not dry.
Dip in the sauce, and enjoy!

Red Wine Roast

This is so effortless, even your husband could do it! (Kidding! Kidding!)

Ingredients

> ½ lb beef roast
> ½ cup red wine
> 1 tbsp salt
> 1 tsp pepper

Instructions

> Put everything in your slow cooker.
> Cook on low for about 10 hours.

Excellent!

Banana-Coconut Cookies

So simple and quick!

Ingredients
> 2 bananas
> ½ cup shredded coconut
> 1 tbsp organic honey (optional)

Directions
> Preheat your oven to 350°F (176°C).
> Slice bananas into a bowl.
> Mash the bananas.
> Add the honey and the coconut.
> Mix together bananas, honey, coconut.
> Drop nine cookies on a sprayed or parchment paper-lined cookie sheet.
> Cook for 15 minutes, and watch them disappear!

Crispy Crackers

Ingredients

1 cup almond or sunflower seed flour
1 egg white
1/8 tsp salt

Directions

Preheat your oven to 325°F (163°C).

In a bowl, mix the ingredients together, forming a dough.

Sandwich the dough between two pieces of parchment paper.

Use a rolling pin to roll the dough to about 1/8" thick. The thinner you make it, the crispier your crackers will be.

Remove the top sheet of paper.

Place the bottom sheet on a cookie sheet.

Use a pizza cutter to score the dough into crackers.

Bake for about 8 to 10 minutes. Remember, the thinner you've made your dough, the faster it will cook. Remove them from the oven when they are golden brown.

What a snap!

Chocolate Turtles

These are amazing!

Ingredients
6 Medjool dates
¾ cup Enjoy Life chocolate chips, melted
48 raw pecan halves

Directions
Cut dates in half lengthwise.
Remove pits.
Using your hands, form each date into a circle shape.
Put the dates, with the open side up, on a cookie sheet lined with parchment paper.
Put four pecan halves, in the shape of a flower, into the center of each date.
In a double boiler, melt the chocolate chips.
Put ½ tsp of the chocolate into a date, and turn it over.
Do the rest of the dates the same way.
Place into the freezer for five minutes.
Keep the chocolate warm.
Remove the dates from the freezer.
Put each into the chocolate to cover its back.
Put back into the freezer for 10 minutes.

Fantastic!

Roasted Figs

These are not only scrumptious, they are beautiful!

Ingredients
    8 figs
    2 tbsp honey
    1 tbsp coconut oil
    ½ tsp vanilla extract

Directions:
    Preheat the oven to 375°F (191°C).
    Wash and dry the figs.
    Cut the tops off. Cut them into quarters,
    lengthwise, leaving the connection at the
    bottom, so that they look like flowers when they
    are laid into your baking dish.
    In a pot, mix and warm the other ingredients.
    Drizzle over the figs.
    Bake for 25 minutes.

Delicious fig flowers!

No-Bake Macaroons

I've said it before, and I'll say it again. I-love-macaroons.

Ingredients
½ cup of coconut oil
½ cup of coconut butter
1 to 1½ cups of unsweetened shredded coconut
3-4 tbsp of maple syrup or honey to taste

Instructions
In a pot, soften the oil and butter.
Remove from heat.
Add the maple syrup or the honey.
Add the coconut until you get the consistency you want
Drop the macaroons, in the desired size and shape, onto a plate.
Pop into the fridge.

I would have to top mine with melted chocolate, but that would be too many ingredients!

Review

I hope you've enjoyed reading this little cookbook. Even more, I hope you'll LOVE eating these delicious dishes!

Enjoy this book?
Please leave a review, and let us know what you liked about this book.

Books by Marjorie Kramer

1. The No-Cook, Skinny, Delicious, Nutritious Overnight Oats in a Jar Cookbook
2. The No-Cook, Skinny, Delicious, Nutritious, Oat Smoothies Cookbook
3. The 4 Ingredients Paleo Cookbook – All The Recipes Have 4 Ingredients or Fewer!
4. The 2 Ingredient Cookbook – All The Recipes Have Only 2 Ingredients!
5. The 2 Ingredient Dessert Cookbook – All the recipes have only 2 ingredients!

6. The 26 Worst Facebook Grammar Mistakes Ever & How to Avoid Them
7. Charting New Territory in ESL – What You Wish Your ESL Book Included

CPSIA information can be obtained at www.ICGtesting.com
Printed in the USA
LVOW10s2054070115

421889LV00038B/2203/P